Fear is living in the land of uncertainty. Trust is living in the land of security found only in the presence of our savior Jesus Christ.

Creatives

Carrie Christopher
CoFounder | lionheartministry.com

Lynne Hudson
Illustrator | lynnehudson.com

Kayla Follin
Graphic Designer | kaylafollin.com

Lindsey Sullivan
Songwriter & Copyeditor | alabasterheart.co

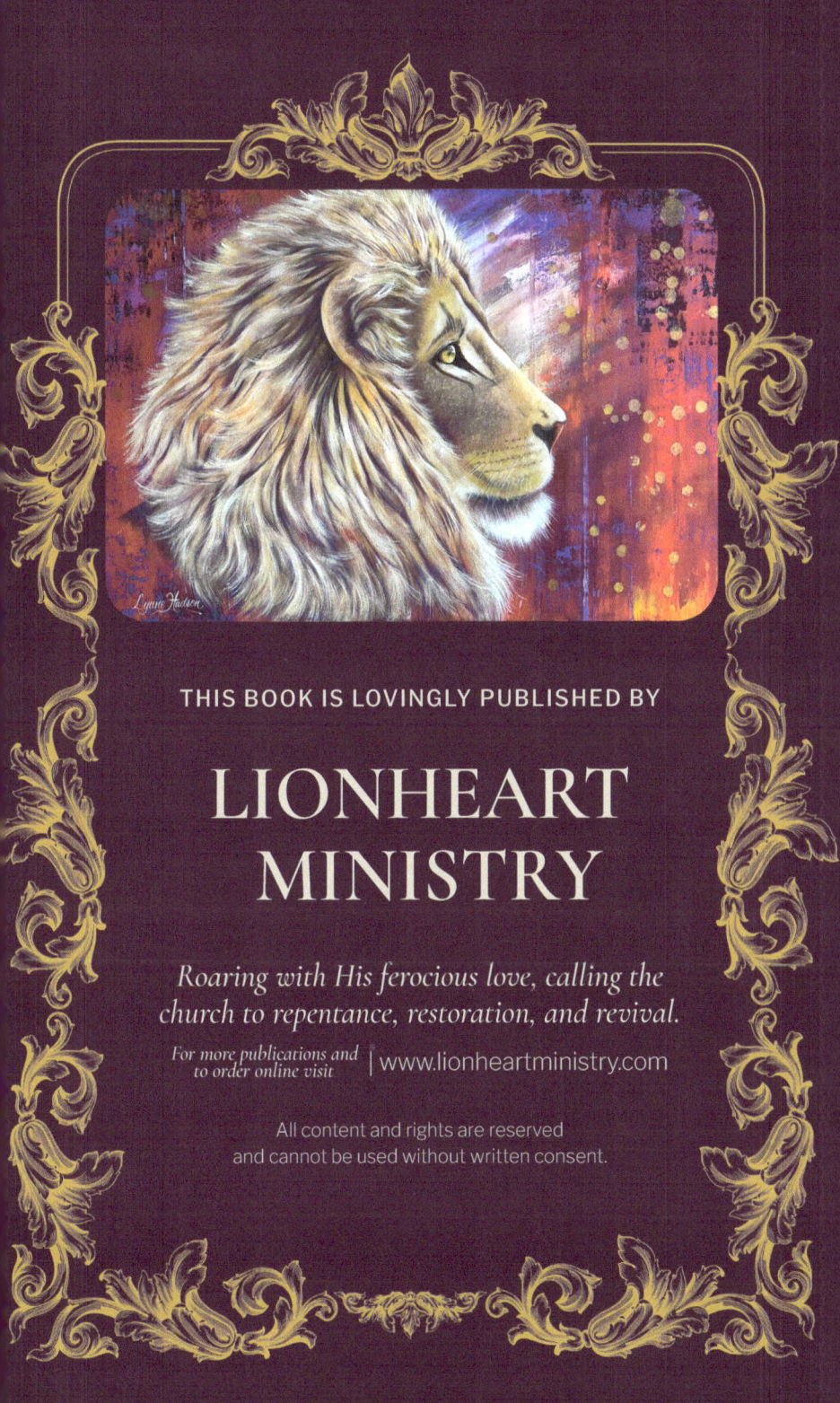

This book is wholeheartedly dedicated and set aside in gratitude and honor toward my beloved husband and in celebration of the lifelong love of God toward my children.

Illustrated by Lynne Hudson

Do Not Fear, Deer One

Written by Carrie Christopher

GOSPEL GOODNESS

You were bought at a price.
1 CORINTHIANS 6:20 (NIV)

DEER ONE,

Our Savior, longing to be with us, was ready to die. He died a death that He did not deserve so that we, who were once held bound to our sins, could be free.

Love enticed Him, His heart wholly given to the Father on our behalf so that we could become heirs with Christ, and sons and daughters reunited with our Father.

Painful fury laid upon our Savior, with waves of destructive sins smothering our sinless spotless Lamb of deliverance.

It was the price that He paid on our behalf, to pay the penalty for our transgressions. We have been freed by the blood of the Lamb—freed by His perfection, artistically woven into His tapestry of plans and purposes for us.

Released from fear. Secured in His love. We no longer have to live in entangled webs of insecurities, doubts and fears. We can surrender our hearts to our God, to our risen Savior and taste the goodness, mercy and power of our triumphant King! Christ rose in power, in victory, and in strength!

May His strength be yours, His victory beholds you. He is waiting for you, and calling you from the depths of heaven, He has named you.

The Son of God who knew no sin, laid down His life for you and me.

May this gift of prospering mercy richly indwell you. May salvation be your song, and Christ be your lifelong companion of hope, communing with the Father of lights.

PENNED IN HIS MERCY,

Carrie Christopher
Author

WELCOME

He makes my feet like the feet of a deer; he causes me to stand on the heights.
PSALM 18:33 (NIV)

Crisp air circulates the morning, as four *does* awake to the rising of the dawn. The group of deer wander into our high grass, choosing a particular tree to gnaw at the bitter leaves. Their brown sleek stature and prominent graceful poise gives me an urge to live among the wild. Beauty dances in the dew drops all around them, pointing to the only One of great glory who could've ever dreamed up the creation of such awe and wonder. One weary doe sits in the wet grass to have her breakfast, chewing and chewing over and over. As we peer out of our windows, they look at us aware of every noise and action. They don't seem to mind that we are staring, but every little thumping noise causes the deer to stop instantly, getting them ready to take flight at any given moment. Yet, God gives us more time to just stare, immersed in the blessed grandeur of His creation. Something startles the littlest one, and their momma says it's time to move. Instantly those lying down rise with determination, and with their pounding hooves they race away. Momma leads the herd back to

DEER ONE

safety. They run fast and gracefully, leaping in mid-air over any obstacles, achieving great heights and bounds of air and beauty. Ah, to only be that free, that graceful, that enabled, my soul churns, longing to be like one. Deer are incredibly beautiful creatures crafted by our good God of grace. May our lives and higher callings be like the blessed deer, enabled to stand on heights of heaven, treading on our fears and willingly carrying the gospel to the ends of the earth, no matter the enemy, the oppositional terrain or any heights of danger! May we stand on mountaintops, trusting our Creator that He made us for this exact moment, positioned and equipped by God with the power in Christ Jesus to stand firm in danger, protected and loved by our Father in heaven.

Do not fear, Deer one
For the Lord your God is here
His protective presence always near

Do not fear, Deer one
Let His perfect love fill every fretful place
Holding and caring for your every burden-filled space

Do not fear, Deer one
Your God roars an intercessory cheer
Over each and every trial and tear

Do not fear, Deer one
Our God disarms your warring foe
He will be with you in power wherever you shall go

Do not fear, Deer one
Submit, surrender and trust
It is your God who gives the enemy a retaliating thrust

Do not fear, Deer one
Watch and you will see
Every one of the lies encircling your mind
   will run away and flee

Do not fear, Deer one
Your God reigns above it all
Indwelling you with His Holy Spirit dove,
   wooing you with His loving call

*I sought the Lord, and he answered me;
he delivered me from all my fears.*
PSALM 34:4 (NIV)

DEER ONE,

Resist the enemy of fear and he will flee from you. Cling to God above all else. His love is for you, mapping out each defining moment of your days to come. He has unfolded the days past to carry a purpose forward, and those days ahead of you will be a radical embarking of seeing God's manifold wisdom cascade over your life. Your Abba Father in heaven loves you purely, wholly and entirely. He will never fail you, nor cause you harm. He is your great avenger who will trample every last lie and accuser in your life. You were made to experience the risen Lord, so retreat into His presence. Tuck your heart away into His tender shelter of refuge.

He is for you, Deer one.

FROM FEAR TO FAITH,

Carrie

The glow of the setting sun

Marks the day ending and the day's work done

I wrestled, I prayed, I sought the Lord in moments of fear

I pondered, I immersed my soul in a God who is really near

It did not come without losses or sacrifices or cost

But He gave back to me an increase and none was lost

I pursued His riches, His ways and the enamor of His totality

And was delivered from my limited understanding of reality

God's wonder keeps me pondering in prayer

Casting every worthless idol away, and every sin snare

The depths of His heart brings healing about

He chases away my every fear, dispersing every lingering doubt

He is a truth teller, a victorious abode

Lifting my earthly striving and heavy burden load

Grace is within my Father, my triumphant King

He puts upon me a promise of redemption and a healing ring

So I will choose to open up my fretting, broken heart

Letting God in to heal me, giving me a new start

Let go, live in love, and turn away from anxious worry

He will heal and redeem without earthly hurry

God your Abba will take care of you

His promises are radically full of grace and true

Call out in your fear and see a God whose banner is delight

Preparing you with His strength, like eagles wings to take flight

They will have no fear of bad news;
their hearts are steadfast, trusting in the Lord.
Their hearts are secure, they will have no fear;
in the end they will look in triumph on their foes.
PSALM 112:7-8 (NIV)

DEER ONE,

Your Father is present, never leaving you nor forsaking you. His promises are trustworthy and true. He tenderly takes your heart and your hand into lands of heavenly purposes. Whisper your pain to the Lord, sing your praises and do not withhold your cares from His presence. Every detail of your life is held and important. He will be your constant security, your everlasting God of hope. When your eyes meet His glorious gaze you will receive peace upon peace. Lavished comfort is yours in His care! Return your gaze and thoughts to Him every moment of the day and be wholly loved.

FROM FEAR TO FAITH,

Carrie

Control perceived is control deceived
Control is a liar, that I can keep contentment near
Control is a lion promising to keep fear here
Jesus is a haven, birthing great truth
Jesus is a provider, pushing past with power-filled proof
Our Father in heaven only requires a heart's release
To accept His plans in trials of darkness, providing overcoming peace
Fear cannot have me, guilt sent to the cross to die
Waves of deliverance rushing to and fro, angels sent from on high
Protection and covering surpassing all knowledge of my own
A banner of love declaring a promise pledge, my Father's care is shown
A covenant, eternally living and lasting forever
It is the lies I'm believing that He will valiantly sever
My God, my refuge, my almighty King
Alarming His troops with His voice, an army to sing
Singing and praising on a battlefield of strife
Declaring His Truth, surrendering my life
I will sing in a place of triumph, I will sing in a place of shame
I will sing of the very mighty love of God rejoicing in His fame
Our God has not forgotten you, nor lost you or let you go
His promises within you assure you with confidence to know
The devil is a roaring lion liar
But his timing is running out, he is doomed to an everlasting fire
I welcome you to follow a God who never fails
Be filled, loved warrior with harvesting victory tales
Tales of truth and grace
Alive and active in every dooming space
My God is a giver, a sure power to deliver
Receive and conceive
Receive and conceive
Only believe, believe, believe

So do not fear, for I am with you;
do not be dismayed, for I am your God.
I will strengthen you and help you;
I will uphold you with my righteous right hand.
ISAIAH 41:10 (NIV)

DEER ONE,

Fear is a liar, a spirit that wants to steal, kill and destroy you. The weapon of fear in your life can be disassembled through confession, repentance and rebuke. Return to the Lord, carrying every anxious thought and paralyzing fear to Him in repentance. Repent for not trusting in His love and then rebuke the father of lies in Jesus' mighty name. Fear promises that past events will reoccur and convince you that pain and suffering are greater than God's redemptive plans for your life. These are all satanic ploys spewed from the father of lies. You will need to war against this beast continually all the days of your life. Tell fear where it needs to stay, at your feet, as you tread upon it as a defeated foe and submit to God in surrender and repentance.

FROM FEAR TO FAITH,

Carrie

Fear do you hear?
You can't live here

My Father's filling love
Gives you a holy shove
You are overcome by His
   mighty dove

Fear do you hear?
You can't live here!

My soul will cling to
   the only power
The love that holds me
   in this appointed hour

Fear do you hear?
You can't live here!

I declare the end of your days
Because at the foot of the
   cross my soul lays

Fear do you hear?
You can't live here

I was made for communion
   with my perfect King
Chosen to be filled with love
   encompassing my heart to sing

Fear do you hear?
You can't live here!

My entire being is set aside
   for the glory of the One
Desiring to reflect the image
   of His heavenly Son

Fear do you hear?
You can't live here!

My Father of truth fills
   me with peace
Charging with love that
   commands fear to cease

Fear you do you hear?
You can't live here!

You spewing father of lies
You are clothed in disguise
You have to leave at the
   sound of His voice
His power over you gives
   you no choice

Fear do you hear?
You can't live here!

The temple of God resides
In the inner place of my being,
   on the inside
So once and for all
You have been cursed
   by the fall
Slither away
You can no longer stay

Submit yourselves, then, to God.
Resist the devil, and he will flee from you.
JAMES 4:7 (NIV)

DEER ONE,

As a little girl I struggled with the enemy coming into my dreams. He would attack me from peaceful rest. I didn't really know how to access God's power yet, nor had I surrendered my life. But a wise counselor told me to pray before falling asleep that God would protect me. So I tried it night after night, and to no avail every single night I cried out to God to protect me, my dreams were literally covered by His blood. The enemy could not interrupt the peace God had for me. These prayers were a small way that I was led to trust God. What I didn't know back in my early childhood years was that the Lord would gift me with prophetic dreams to lead me. As a Christ-loving adult, I receive the Lord's leading through dreams regularly. This is one common form of companionship with Him. You see, the enemy wanted to rob me of these encounters prophetically with the Lord! So if you're reading this and are commonly attacked at night by the enemy, then simply pray for His protection. Surrender your life, confess your sins and then ask God to release prophetic dreams. Those who are most attacked in the night hour are usually those whom He has chosen to flood with His presence! Being carried into His heavenly realm in the night hour is one of my greatest blessings on this earth!

Dream with your Savior!

FROM FEAR TO FAITH,

Carrie

I will choose not to fear
But to hear
Hear His voice above the waves
Tuning into the only
   voice that saves

I will choose not to fear
But to hear
To hear His loving sound
His word in my soul,
   where I am wholly found

I will choose not to fear
But to hear
Entering into the depths of
   His intentional love
Cooing softly my deliverance
   as I now rise above

I will choose not to fear
But to hear
The thunder of Your word,
   above all of the lies
Entranced by the heavenly
   encounter of Your presence
   displayed in the skies

I will choose not to fear
But to hear
Of the victory reigning right
   behind this road of dark
I can hear choirs of angels
   singing of His holy
   retaliation mark

I will choose not to fear
But to hear
The bellowing of Your love
   coming down in streams of
   great glory
Armed with the powerful hand
   of God, this isn't the end
   of my story

I will choose not to fear
But to hear
The overflowing loving
   graciousness of Your call
Into the courts of Your
   compassion I humbly
   submit and fall

I will choose not to fear
But to hear
Your voice testifying Your
   faithfulness and care
You will never forsake me or
   leave me in darkness to bear

Come to me, all you who are weary and burdened, and I will give you rest. Take my yoke upon you and learn from me, for I am gentle and humble in heart, and you will find rest for your souls. For my yoke is easy and my burden is light.
MATTHEW 11:28-30 (NIV)

DEER ONE,

Fear is a robber, wanting to control the heritage set aside for you in Christ Jesus. Push into peace. Jesus promises peace to those He loves! Fear produces anxiety, fret, worry and beyond! But God's waterfall of His love chases it out with wonder! When fear begins to leave, you will notice the fruit of peace. Peace transcends beyond any of our understanding or comprehension. It is a place of refuge, of secure trust and intimacy with the Lord. Peace promises His presence, and in His presence is fullness of joy. Practice His presence and seek His face and you will be kissed with all abounding peace. Your heart will no longer war against lies in this place, but it will settle, nestle into the comforting, secure arms of your savior. You are safe in the Lord. He is your protector. Nothing will ever be able to separate you from His love. He loves you yesterday, today and tomorrow, and into all eternity. His transcending love will lead you forward into a pathway of peace in His presence.

FROM FEAR TO FAITH,

Carrie

From fear to freedom
I will not fear
But revere
I will look to the eyes of my King
Boldly proclaim and sing
This fear that is trying to silence me
Will run at the name of Jesus and flee
The reassurance of His love
Will renounce fear from above
Fear will scamper away as a weapon rendered lost
Filling me with hope and purging my sin dross
Waves of prayer power shall roll
Held by angels gathering a victory incense bowl
The Lord has not left me, nor forgotten my pain
God has filled my soul with a victory and Holy Spirit gain
I will not tremble in the presence of intimidating fear
My God almighty will deliver and tenderly draw near
My story isn't over and these lies have not won
The Father has kept me, through the blood of His son
The sovereignty of God will assure me at last
His love everlasting, triumphantly surpassed
Victory is rising
As fear is demising

There is no fear in love. But perfect love drives out fear, because fear has to do with punishment. The one who fears is not made perfect in love.
1 JOHN 4:18 (NIV)

DEER ONE,

If I am honest, I have wasted days imprisoned by the fear of man. I don't quite understand the intricacies of when it took hold of my life. But at the core of me, I desire for constant peace, love, grace and mercy in all of my relationships so I get ensnared by the false lord of man. Where the spirit of the Lord is there is freedom. Sometimes we have to step back from friendships and evaluate if they are fruit-filled from the Lord and if we are guarding our hearts with the much needed counsel of the Lord. You are wholly accepted in Christ, and perfectly loved. You do not need to spend all your days pleasing people when you should be focused on serving the Lord! Friendship with God's people should bring freedom and sing of His love. Confess your sin of fear of man. This is deeply embedded into insecure notions of who you are! You are His prized possession, a child of the most high, favored, set aside and you can rest in that love and operate in the calling of who He made you to be! Be free, deer one!

FROM FEAR TO FAITH,

Carrie

Anxiety and fear promised me
Perceived control
Anxiety and fear led me to believe
My way was the solution
Anxiety and fear stole
My surrender and my yes to God
Anxiety and fear clouded His voice and fed my sin
They came to steal all and destroy
To stifle His hope, peace and life within me
To feed my pride, to be the ruler of my own soul
It felt like a trap, a snare with no way out
Discontentment began to breed despair
Complaining, grumbling and my aching heart became my constant
My heart was clothed with darkness, joy overridden by fear
But God
My heart cries out in confession
The desire to be free from what gripped me
Deliverance began as I humbled myself in prayer
And the Lord's word gave me three solutions to build my soul
Prayer, petitions and thanksgiving
May prayer bring our hearts into His presence
   with deep abandoned trust
May our petitions cast our cares on a God who loves
May thanksgiving drift our eyes away from darkness into light
The repetition of my soul,
   His rescue for me shouting
Prayer, petitions and thanksgiving
Each there ringing
Glorious truth above the lies
Saving my heart from a soul sapping season
Believing the truth that in all trials, we are overcomers
   marked by the blood of Jesus
We shall win

Do not be anxious about anything, but in every situation, by prayer and petition, with thanksgiving, present your requests to God. And the peace of God, which transcends all understanding, will guard your hearts and your minds in Christ Jesus.
PHILIPPIANS 4:6-7 (NIV)

DEER ONE,

Seek the Lord with your entire heart. Resist the enemy and he will flee from you. Fear trembles at the sight of your surrender to God. God is able and tenderly desires to conquer your every foe. Trust in the Lord with your whole heart and lean not on your own understanding. God will fill your every need with His power, love and triumphant presence. God is a Father of hope. Fear likes to create hopelessness and oppression carries defeat. Your God is able to deliver you from every deadly affliction, every form of mockery, every evidence of lawlessness. God is for you, His kindness leads you to repentance. Open your heart to receive His wholehearted loving will. Stand up for justice and the oppressed. Know you are loved.

FROM FEAR TO FAITH,
Carrie

Peace, I am told, is His presence to be bold
Courage, I have seen, is understanding by
   His Holy Spirit alone shall I lean
Healing to be received links to promises believed
The abiding power that I know is marked
   as the only path I shall go
Fear to be released rests on all striving to be ceased
Heaven to be kissed disarms what satan has hissed
Faith to be held allows lies to be repelled
Promises to be received linger on truths believed
Glory to be awakened brings repentance shaken
A loving Father's lullaby soothes my heart's inner cry
Love cursing fear, wipes away my every tear

Have I not commanded you? Be strong and courageous. Do not be afraid; do not be discouraged, for the LORD your God will be with you wherever you go.
JOSHUA 1:9 (NIV)

DEER ONE,

Your Father's voice should call and tell you the way to go! Abiding in the presence of God is a relational wisdom-filled voice of love, light and mercy! As you grow closer to the Lord's living love and reigning voice, you will be able to discern which path to take. You may not choose every right path and that is ok! Do not fear failure or making a mistake because I have made countless poor choices and have seen our faithful God redeem them all! And what is redemption of all things anyways? I see redemption as the Lord's overflowing grace covering my every sinful or wrong choice! God is a shepherd teacher, so He is gently leading with correction. We learn through our stumbling actions and through the loving consequences of sin! God will never abandon us. His voice is like a spotlight in the darkness and even if we shall turn away, He will leave the 99 sheep to come and find us! The key is to stay open to His Holy Spirit! Don't ever forsake spending time with the Lord, because then, my friend, you will wander, get hurt and eventually feel lost. Stay close to Jesus' heart. Spend time with him reading, praying, singing and attending church. Have friendship with believers so you can each strengthen one another. Do not give up. Eventually you will hear His voice. It takes practice to learn how to receive from Him and die to your pride. We are all sinners, weak and weary, but not left to ourselves to figure it out. God is the best father we will ever experience and His patience and pursuit of us will never die! So you don't have to live in a pressurized bubble of insecurity and fear of failure! Jump with Jesus. He will catch you. Surrender your life and love to Him above all else!

FROM FEAR TO FAITH,
Carrie

Fear be gone

Release this tender fawn

You've been a bully brute

You've harassed me at dawn with an illegal loot

You kept me tossing to and fro

Lying there lost, believing I had nowhere to go

You backed me into a cruel deceiving corner

Promising me the fate of a forsaken mourner

Your venomous lies have shaken me to the core

Your luring voice mimicking a wild wicked boar

But the time has come, where my God shows up

He speaks passionately "enough is enough"

You may not have me, you may not lead me

Your violent presence may have blinded me to see

But now your day has come to an abrupt end

My God comes with loving healing, mercy to mend

All of your destruction and all of your lies

Our God has come to speak of your doomed demise

He is my Abba Father, a God of peace

All attacks from the spirit of fear have to cease

I am comforted, held and nourished with His pleasure

His everlasting love reaches the clouds beyond height to measure

Finally free as a grace-filled restored fawn

By Your Spirit I am led and wholly drawn

Therefore tell the people: This is what the LORD Almighty says: "Return to me," declares the LORD Almighty, "and I will return to you," says the LORD Almighty.
ZECHARIAH 1:3 (NIV)

DEER ONE,

This life can sometimes be brutal. We can get hurt by our own sin and the consequences of others' sins. I wish I could tell you that you will never get hurt and that life is perfect. But I would be lying. Life is broken and hard, and there are many things and people that will hurt you. The reassuring hope is that your healer, Jesus will mend all of your wounds! He actually causes all evil to work together for your good. Part of growing in trust and love in the Lord is through the bitter way of suffering! Whenever you doubt this, just look at how Jesus endured the cross for us! If we desire to partake in His glory then we also will suffer for His namesake! Your whole life is intended to worship God, to experience His love, to give His love and to go and tell others about this love! I promise you, life in the Spirit is never boring! God uses his Holy Spirit to speak in miraculous ways through dreams, visions, words, and other believers! Every time God speaks, I think, "Wow this is just a miracle!" Modern day movies and books try to write stories that captivate and excite you. Let me tell you, living a life full of the Spirit crushed all the earthly ways of trying to live a life full of awesome wonder and joy. It is God's story, and the way He wants to speak to you is better than you can ever imagine! So don't stop chasing Him with your whole heart, you'll be captivated in the awe and wonder of His presence and you'll never want to leave! When I spend time with Jesus and the Spirit comes upon me, I literally never want to go back to earth. He keeps me coming for more and more of His heavenly encounters! Know that you are loved!

FROM FEAR TO FAITH,
Carrie

Every scar will be turned to a praise

We will worship the Lord in the travail and the best of our days

Every obstacle becomes a trust walk

Expecting the Lord to reign, deliver and gather His flock

Every victory will bring us joy to soar

On the wings of faith eagles opening heaven's door

Every tear will be made into a new song

Giving glory to our Savior all the day long

Ours stories are unfinished, with more pages to be written

It is the radiant face of our Father that will never grow weary or smitten

He looks upon us with love, grace and mercy showering

Faith once feeble now strengthened, over our enemies towering

Grace blankets our every move

God's love overcoming our fear with His grace to soothe

Victories triumphing over our greatest losses

Embalmed with His riches and healed from our anxious tosses

Now the Lord is the Spirit, and where the Spirit of the Lord is, there is freedom.
2 CORINTHIANS 3:17 (NIV)

DEER ONE,

I share this testimony of a six year old boy. Oh, did the Lord have plans for this child. One evening the fear battle raged between heaven and earth and the child asked his parents to pray for him. After praying, the child had an encounter that will be sung over him as a declaration of love for the entirety of his life. As he laid down his weary head, he heard triumphant angels singing over him. Angels! An actual choir of angels. If you're wrestling with fear, cry out to God and ask Him to reveal His almighty outpouring of love to you. Ask to hear angels singing, or to be filled with comforting scriptures, or to hear His heavenly troops, or the Father's voice, or to see the Lord in a much needed vision. God is not a distant complacent God, He is an actively loving, grace giving, enemy shoving powerful King! Go to the mountain with Him, deer one, and you'll see fear flee!

FROM FEAR TO FAITH,
Carrie

His love is constant and pure
Steadfast and sure
Redeeming and bright
Full of power and might
A mighty love-filled ocean
Filled with tangible commotion
A well so deep and wide
Lavishing His grace
   deeply inside
A love embrace holding us tight
Restoring our wholeness
   and healing our sight
A love that is constant,
   endless and firm
Having no expiration term
A song of truth-filled words
Brighter than even the voices
   of the birds
A care that is urgent and quick
One that answers speedily
   to heal the sick
A love sent to redeem the lost
Ushering us into His arms
   no matter the cost
He is embracing us with
   arms open wide
Showering His mighty
   love inside
He bestows upon us the riches
   of His great glory
Heralding His love through the
   depths of our story
He leads us through the valley
   of the shadow of death
Rebuking our fears with His
   Holy Spirit's breath
A lover hushing comfort
   over our souls
Carrying every burden
   tenderly in incense bowls
The richness of His
   compassion and mercy too
Coloring our trials with
   a radiant hue
Giving us resilient strength
   to climb any mountain
Welcoming us to drink
   from His glory fountain
Refreshing and pure
Trustworthy and sure
Our Father's love
Shed from heaven above

I have loved you with an everlasting love;
I have drawn you with unfailing kindness.
JEREMIAH 31:3 (NIV)

DEER ONE,

Oh, the abounding, abiding, all-encompassing love of Jesus! He has freedom plans for you. His deliverance plan for your life to rip the generational sin curse of fear from your heart is apparent and set aside for an amazing display of His glory! Fear doesn't get the final say in your life. In fact, the Lord has set aside this glory story of deliverance to literally proclaim His fame! The Lord is calling you higher, up the mountain of great travail for the glorious heights of freedom! You have to keep climbing with Christ and never ever stop! Remember the story of Moses. He got to see God from a burning bush. Let me tell you my warrior friend, God has so much more planned for you. If your faith feels feeble and stagnant, get ready. A wildfire of revival is about to spread on our lands. And those who cling to the living hope of Jesus are called to become just like the disciples in the book of Acts! You are being prepared to be launched into lands of the living God! Lands of miracles, where prophecies unfold and tell of the great story of old. Where baptism in the Holy Spirit will flourish for believers who are ready to leave their old lives behind! You, my friend, are called, chosen, and you are going to prosper this land with the rich vastness of the presence of God! Are you ready to carry His presence to the end of the ages? Keep climbing!

FROM FEAR TO FAITH,

Carrie

Faith over fear so I can hear

Faith over fear to humbly revere

Faith over fear as His presence is near

Faith over fear to wipe away every tear

Faith over fear into heaven's gates I peer

Faith over fear into mountains grandeur and sheer

Faith over fear as teaching truths become clear

Faith over fear as bold impartations appear

Faith over fear as I enter into the Holy Spirit's sphere

Faith over fear as I tremble in repentance while angels cheer

Faith over fear as I surrender and by His grace persevere

Faith over fear as I tread on heights of heaven
   as a brave and bold deer

He replied, "Because you have so little faith. Truly I tell you, if you have faith as small as a mustard seed, you can say to this mountain, 'Move from here to there,' and it will move. Nothing will be impossible for you."
MATTHEW 17:20 (NIV)

DEER ONE,

Let it all go—all your earthly striving. Abide in the power of the shadow of the Most High and be saved from the oppression of fear. Accept the will of Jesus' death on the cross as the ultimate and final payment for your sin. Perfection is false in this broken world. But when you know your Father in heaven, spending time with Him, listening to His heart and contemplating His Word, you will be changed. The transfiguration of Moses was manifested because He spent time with God on the mountain. So, Deer One, climb the mountain of adversity into His presence and you too will be transformed. You will carry His presence to the very end of the ages, into the lands of the nations. But this means you will have to prepare for battle. Every faithful soldier has to fight to conquer territories. God desires a people who love Him with their whole hearts, the entirety of their beings. Those who know the radical love of the Lord, love the Lord. And those who love the Lord love others because His love indwells the innermost being, a sacred place and space of the presence of the Holy Spirit.

This is war. Fear is fret. Fretting only tends to evil. Resist the evil one, repent of your sins and be transformed on the mountaintop of transfiguration and redemption. God is enough to win all your battles and fill all your hungry heart spaces.

FROM FEAR TO FAITH,
Carrie

PROPHETIC POWER

PROPHETIC DESCRIPTIONS BY LYNNE HUDSON

The flow of the sky captures God's glory striking the deer and encapsulating him. The glory shines through the deer, causing this grounding shadow. The purple hills are the majesty of his righteousness. His antlers represent the overshadowing love of the Father.

— Lynne Hudson

There is a vulnerability with the young doe eating the leaves on his own, while the others are in the background, comforted by their mothers love. But we are never alone, our Father is always there. He has sent

manna from heaven with the dew drops on the leaves representing Heaven's blessings. There is no need to worry, His provision is all around. He blankets us with His protection. — Lynne Hudson

The glory and light is shining down with the guidance of the Holy Spirit through His loving call. Be ushered out of the darkness and into His light. Be filled with the living waters as you stand in His wells of love. Look to the Holy Spirit. Feel His peace. Breathe in the tranquility.

— Lynne Hudson

Rest in His love for you. You are between the past and the purpose of moving forward into the future, into the plans He has for you. Rest in His wisdom. Tuck your heart away in His tender shelter of refuge. Be still, sit, ponder, wait and trust in the Lord. Unclutter your life and focus on His thoughts and His way.

— Lynne Hudson

The glow of the sunset radiates onto your being. Jesus' sacrifice is evident with the sky's contrast of rich red. The eagle is flying high, releasing freedom over you, giving you God's strength. Look to the heavens, believing in God's promises. You may seem alone but God is all around you fulfilling your heart's desires. You are surrounded by God's majesty—the beauty of His love as it showers down upon you.

— Lynne Hudson

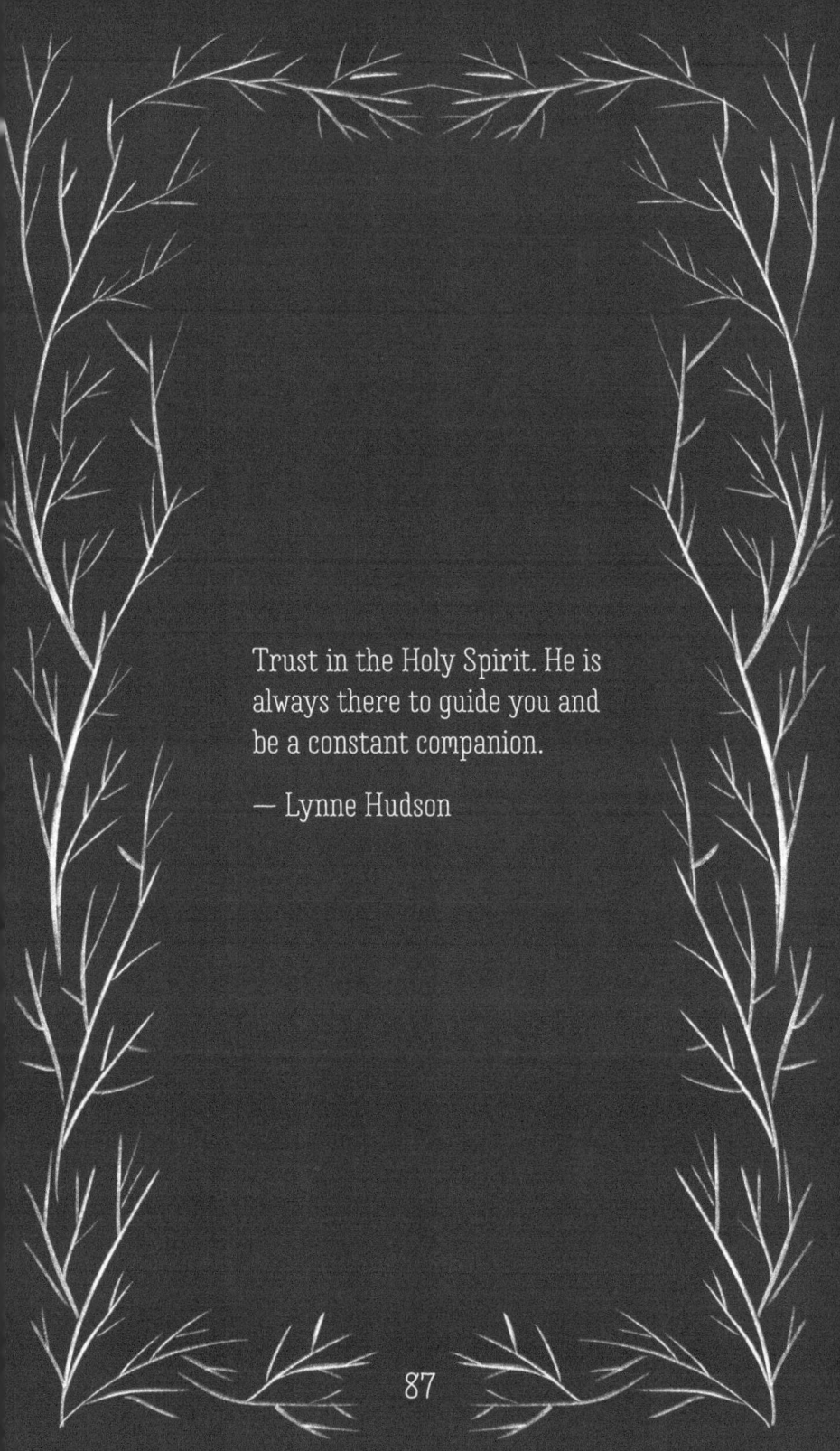

Trust in the Holy Spirit. He is always there to guide you and be a constant companion.

— Lynne Hudson

Don't look back! Don't dwell on the past. You can see a path in the distance. This is where you have come from, now look forward. There is a bright new future. Orange for the courage

to walk this new path. You are in a clearing, a clearing out of the old. In the distance there are bright colors. This is the bright future God has for you. — Lynne Hudson

The dark side of the painting is the control. Jesus is the golden glory side, representing a haven of His peace, protection, and deliverance. His covering is in the branches that bend over and create a roof of protection. Follow a God that never fails. You are on a mission, flowing with God's grace as His steps lead you toward the light of Jesus. The red leaves represent the blood of Jesus, the cross. Receive and conceive!

—Lynne Hudson

The darkness of fear is crippling when you are at war against the enemy. But it can be overcome by accepting Jesus with your whole heart. With His love it falls like a light rain, touching and healing the pain and fear. Stand tall upon the fear and the lies.

—Lynne Hudson

Step into the full embrace of God's love with rainbow promises. The Father's fulfilling love is encompassing your heart to sing. Let God melt and blend your heart with His colors pouring into your soul. The flooding down is the healing joyous pink seeping into your righteousness in the Kingdom. Hallelujah! Water is filling you up, refreshing you. Take a step into His fullness of love, where you belong.

—Lynne Hudson

Walk through enemy attacks knowing you have the mighty sovereign protection of the Father.

—Lynne Hudson

Little one, look up to the Father for comfort and protection. Feel His love, His safety. The Lord is your light. Look around, look for His glory in

every situation. He has you in the palm of His hand. Feel the peace surrounding you as you gaze into His reflections. — Lynne Hudson

Hear His voice above the waves. The waves are His ever-present refreshing sound. Behold His glory in the skies as the calling of His love is coming down in streams of light and awe. The victory is yours. This is the freedom from fear represented by the eagle.

—Lynne Hudson

Drink in His rich nourishing blessings of peace. We are reflecting His image. Our glory is shining brightly and the veil has been lifted. We are what we see in the mirror. 2 Cor. 3:18 TPT, "Now we can all draw close to him with the veil removed from our faces. And with no veil we all become like mirrors who brightly reflect the glory of the Lord Jesus." Amen!

—Lynne Hudson

Be saturated with the gold of the Holy Spirit filling you up with His victory. There is freedom of the Spirit, joy, glory, and a new breath of life. Be in gentle wonder and innocence of His mighty love and power.

—Lynne Hudson

When being freed from fear of man there is a purity of freedom, a purity of healing, a purity of being set free from these shackles. Push through the fear of man with new budding life around you.

—Lynne Hudson

God is still doing a work, finishing your story, healing, and building confidence. Not all of the pieces are put together, not all of the story is finished. Stand in the refreshing water. The distant

future is one of beauty and God's plans, a journey to the unknown. Even the sky looks like a jigsaw that reflects in the water. You are surrounded by God's hand in it all. — Lynne Hudson

Step out from the darkness, from the fear and the anxiety through prayer and thanksgiving. Drift your eyes away from darkness and into the light. The soft rays behind are the reminder that God is always there to overcome our fears and the lies if we trust in Him and surrender. The moss is a reminder—don't get comfortable with the darkness. The vines are the new beginnings and life ahead.

—Lynne Hudson

Embrace the love and peace of the Father. The Father tenderly comforts His young, pushing back the darkness of fear. The sapling represents new budding life. There is hope.

—Lynne Hudson

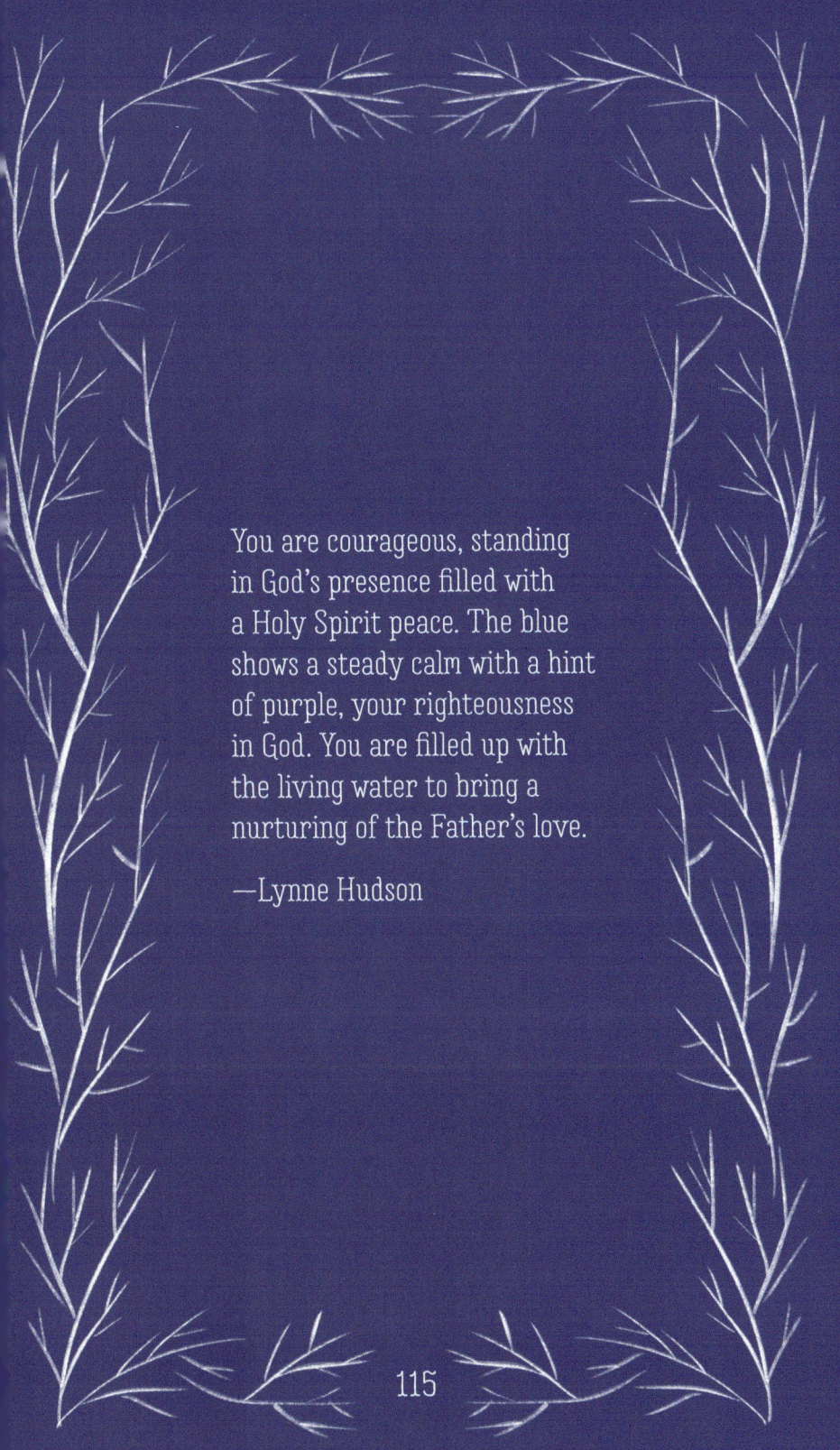

You are courageous, standing in God's presence filled with a Holy Spirit peace. The blue shows a steady calm with a hint of purple, your righteousness in God. You are filled up with the living water to bring a nurturing of the Father's love.

—Lynne Hudson

Drink from the living water as it tumbles down to refill the ever-living stream. The Good Shepherd leads us by tranquil streams to replenish us. There is much darkness around but when we focus on His life and His love we are filled with His life and love. The Holy Spirit hovers. He is the key. You are highlighted in this darkness, and there is more abundance of growth from where the stream is coming. This is the path to take, so follow His lead.

—Lynne Hudson

The Father is looking out, keeping watch over His child. This is our Father, always caring and looking out for us. His child is so precious and innocent.

This is how our Father sees us. He is there bringing us peace through His presence.
— Lynne Hudson

The vines are trying to strangle, to hold back and imprison, but God. You have been shaken to the core, but God. God comes with loving healing mercy to mend and as you receive this, you are filled with His unshakeable strength and love. The simple peace and joy returns. The joy to appreciate the simple wonders of God as He blesses you with His touches from heaven. A butterfly is a majestic act of His kindness as He blesses you to face another day of this battle. The butterfly is your freedom. Focus on your Abba Father. You are as free as a grace-filled restored fawn and by His Spirit you are led and wholly drawn. You are like a beautiful sunrise awakening to a new day, a new season.

—Lynne Hudson

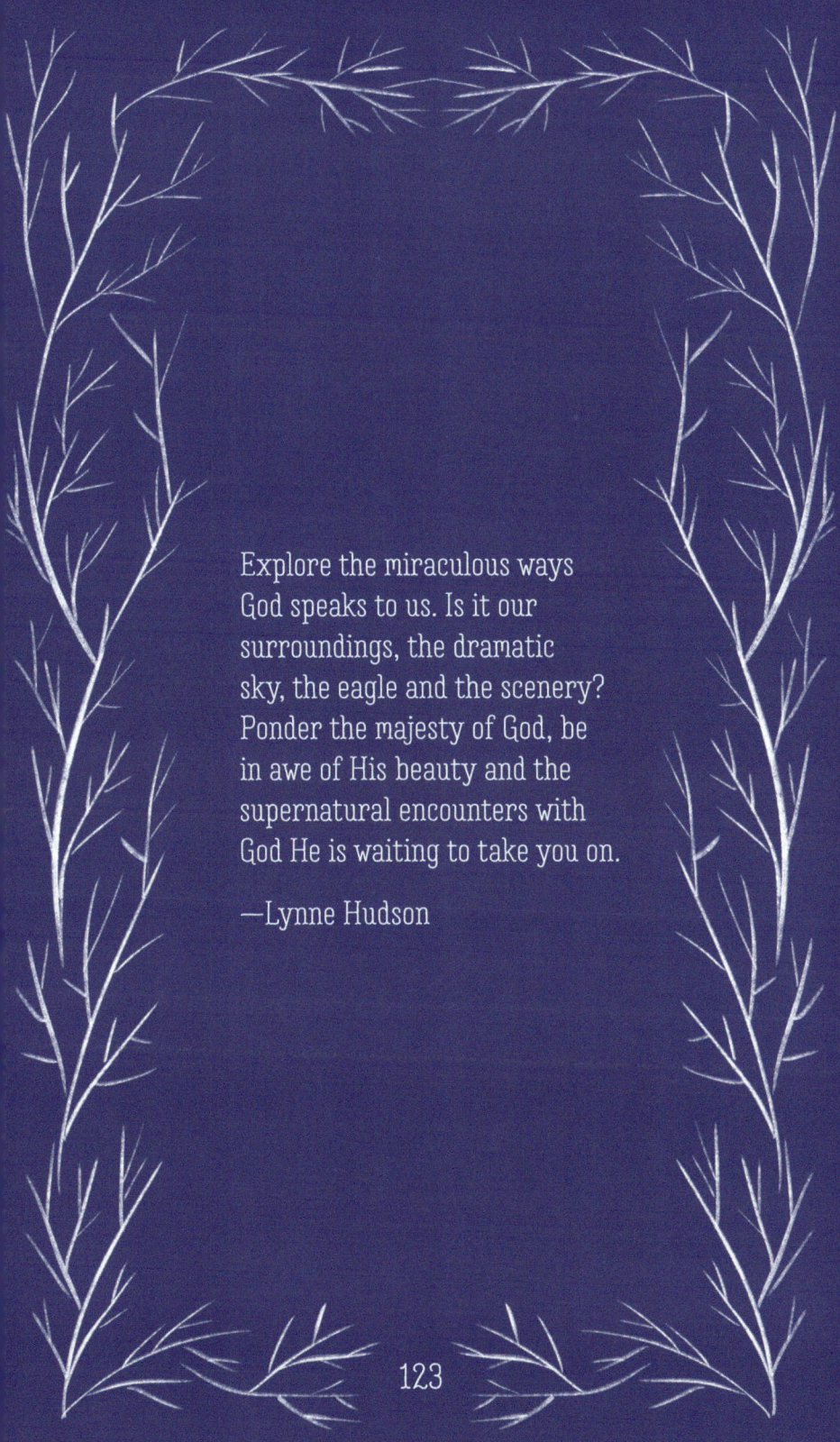

Explore the miraculous ways God speaks to us. Is it our surroundings, the dramatic sky, the eagle and the scenery? Ponder the majesty of God, be in awe of His beauty and the supernatural encounters with God He is waiting to take you on.

—Lynne Hudson

I felt led to paint the deer blue-green, as there is a purity in this color. The color is draining down onto the pages, pouring out the tears we have shed to solidify our story. The pages are still being written, and the story is never over. The blue is the Word. As we go through our own story we are given courage from the Word to fulfill our destiny. The pages are stained with our emotions. The path is gold, representing God's glory testifying to our own personal testimony. The ever-present path is orange to give us the courage to keep going so our book is written, leaving a legacy for others. The eagles have flown to give us strength and open the doors of heaven. The pink clouds are the buoyancy of joy surrounding us through our victories.

—Lynne Hudson

Come to the Father with childlike faith. He paints a picture of such delight when He speaks to us. Have a joyous innocence and surrender to His tender breath of peace. The budding flowers are the atmosphere of an abundance of love and freedom that He showers over us as He speaks and we only need to open our own hearts to be touched by His glorious loving heart.

—Lynne Hudson

Be Still. God showcases His beauty through nature. As we quiet ourselves, we reflect on the magnitude of who God is and how He brings everything together for our good. We need only to trust and know that He has it all planned. So be still and know that He is in control and He has our lives

in His hands. The birds don't worry about their next meal, so why should we wrestle with anxiety for not knowing the future? The doe ponders the majesty of God's creation. The dew drops are the heavenly living water replenishing our dry souls—kisses from heaven. — Lynne Hudson

Stand in the deep water of His love. A well so deep and wide—brighter than even the voices of the birds. He leads us through the valley of death. Meander your way into the light and the bright story that God has for you. He is coloring our trials with a radiant hue as the colors merge from the waters into the skies, giving us resilient strength to climb those mountains again and again, and surrounding us with His welcoming drink from His glory fountain.

—Lynne Hudson

Climb the mountain. The Lord is calling you higher up the mountain of great travail for the glorious heights of freedom. His background is God's glory shining and powerful. God's glory is on fire, like explosions when a bushfire crackles and bursts. From your angle, the situation may look impossible to climb but nothing is impossible when we cling to the living hope of Jesus. Keep climbing!

—Lynne Hudson

Take my hand, receive and walk with me. Heaven's gates await with angels with bold impartations of the Holy Spirit. With faith step out and overcome fear. Your shadow merges with the whitest of snow. The saints are waving you on with celebration.

—Lynne Hudson

Stand in the shadow of the cross, the power of the almighty sacrifice Jesus laid down for us to receive this healing from being bound to fear. It is finished, it is finished! Move the mountain through your faith, stand tall and receive, like Moses did, all the glory and magnificence of God's presence. Be transformed! The blue is the complete healing from fear. The cross is orange, giving us courage to conquer our battles. The cross is transparent because there are no barriers between us and the Lord's love.

—Lynne Hudson

There is a move of the Spirit in our lives. God goes before us and dramatically paints our picture. The colors are interacting mightily, and there is a celebration in the heavens. His children have reunited. They are on level

ground and no longer need to climb. They have reached the top and are at peace. There is a stillness on the ground where they tread. The glory is all around them. The healing has taken place. — Lynne Hudson

A song by Lindsey Sullivan

Don't fear, dear one
Rest in my arms
I want to hold you
I want to hold you close

My presence is a shield
Keeping you from harm
No one can touch you here
You're safe within in my guard

Don't fear, dear one
Rest in my arms
I want to hold you
I want to hold you close

Let my perfect love
Wrap around your heart
Driving out the fear
As you melt into my arms

Don't fear, dear one
Rest in my arms
I want to hold you
I want to hold you close
So come into my arms

SCAN THE QR CODE TO LISTEN TO THE SONG!

www.ingramcontent.com/pod-product-compliance
Lightning Source LLC
Chambersburg PA
CBHW041453010526
44107CB00013B/1029